Square Lamps

PUBLISHED BY:

Cliffside Studio
Made in the USA

ISBN 0-9641597-6-7

Copyright, 2002, 2013, Alex Spatz

INTRODUCTION

"Square Lamps" is intended for medium to advanced hobbyists who have made copper foil panels and perhaps simple lamps. It incorporates more complex designs in the panels and provides more experience in lamp-building before moving on to lampshades with curved panels. Some of the designs have one panel repeated four times, while others have two panels that alternate and when put together, forming a scene on two sides. There are three sizes of lampshades that can be made with these designs, and an optional top crown is included in this book. The 12" lampshades can be made with a 2 3/4" square vase cap as shown on the cover of this book or a spider, while the 14" and 16" lampshades only use a spider.

ENLARGING THE DESIGNS

The designs in this book can be made into 12" sq., 14" sq. or 16" sq. lampshades. First, remove the template page in the center of the book. Next, trace the outline of the size lampshade you wish to make on a sheet of paper. Then enlarge your chosen design to fit the outline using a projector or photocopier. If you use a photocopier you will have to copy half of the design per sheet of paper. Use the percentages below to enlarge your design to the desired size.

> 12" lampshade - 120%
> 14" lampshade - 140% or 120% plus 117%
> 16" lampshade - 160% or 120% plus 120% plus 111%

LAMPSHADE CONSTRUCTION

It is very important to make all the panels the same shape. If they are off even a little bit it will show up when you begin to assemble the panels together. Trace the panel outline very carefully on a sheet of stiff cardboard, then cut the panel shape out of the cardboard. Lay the cardboard on a piece of plywood and fasten wood strips around it to make a template for soldering the panels together.

When you are ready to assemble the panels, begin by setting two of them up on a flat surface. You will need a heavy object on which to lean them while you line up the edges and tack them at the top, middle and bottom. Repeat with the last two panels. Tack the vase cap or spider in place to give the lampshade rigidity. Apply masking tape to the outside edges of the panels you have just tacked together. Carefully lay the lampshade on its side and solder all of the inside edges between the panels. Remove the masking tape and solder the outside edges of the lampshade. It will be necessary to prop it up on a box or something similar so that the edges are level. When the edges are soldered, finish soldering the vase cap or spider. The bottom edges can be tinned with solder or finished with "U" shape zinc came.

LAMP BASES

Select a style of base that you feel is appropriate for your lampshade. Base and harp sizes are shown below.

> 12" lampshade - 10" to 11" base/7" to 71/2" harp
> 14" lampshade - 12" to 13" base/8" to 81/2" harp
> 16" lampshade - 14" to 15" base/9" to 91/2" harp

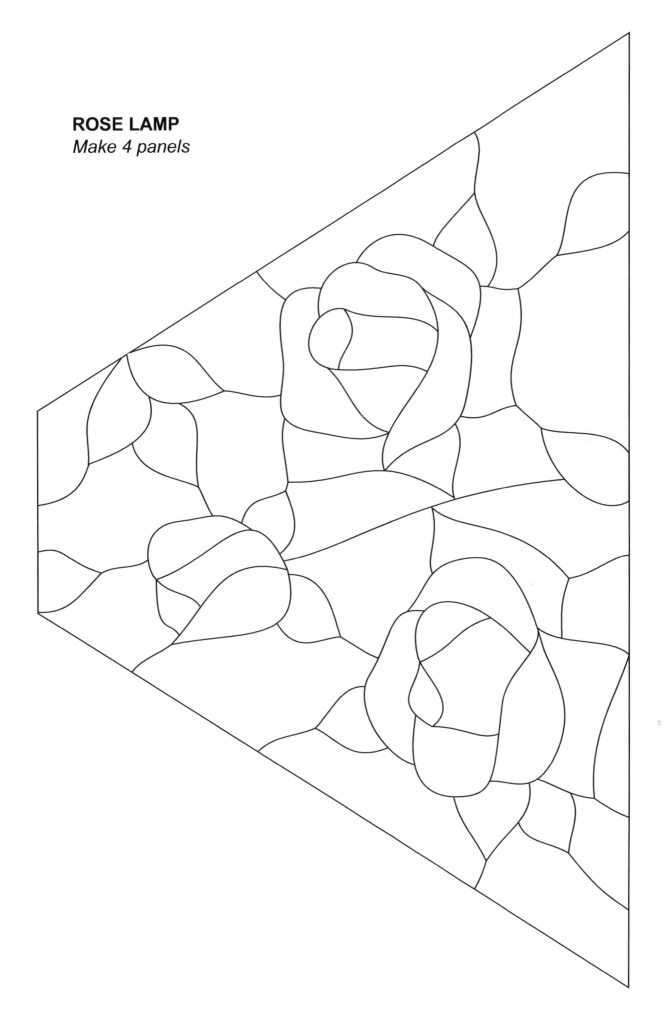

ROSE LAMP
Make 4 panels

1

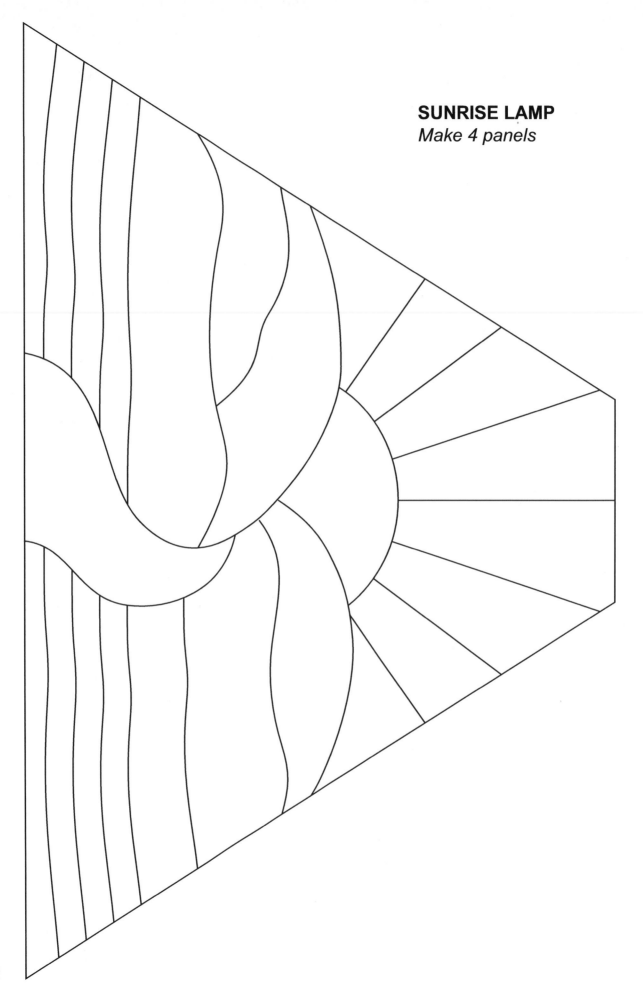

SUNRISE LAMP
Make 4 panels

2

TULIPS LAMP
Make 4 panels

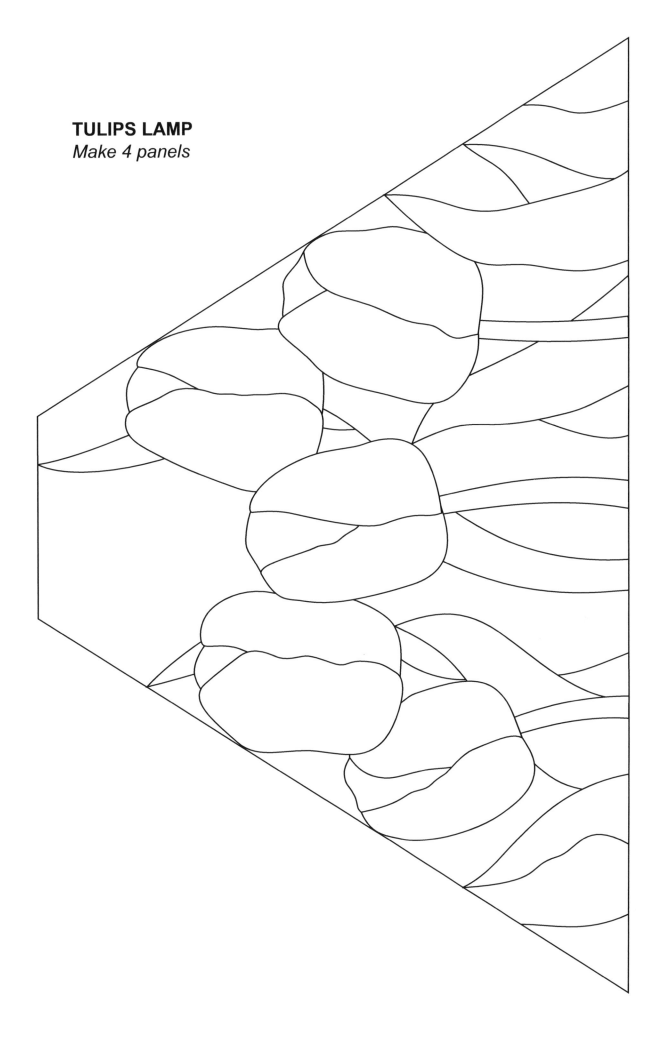

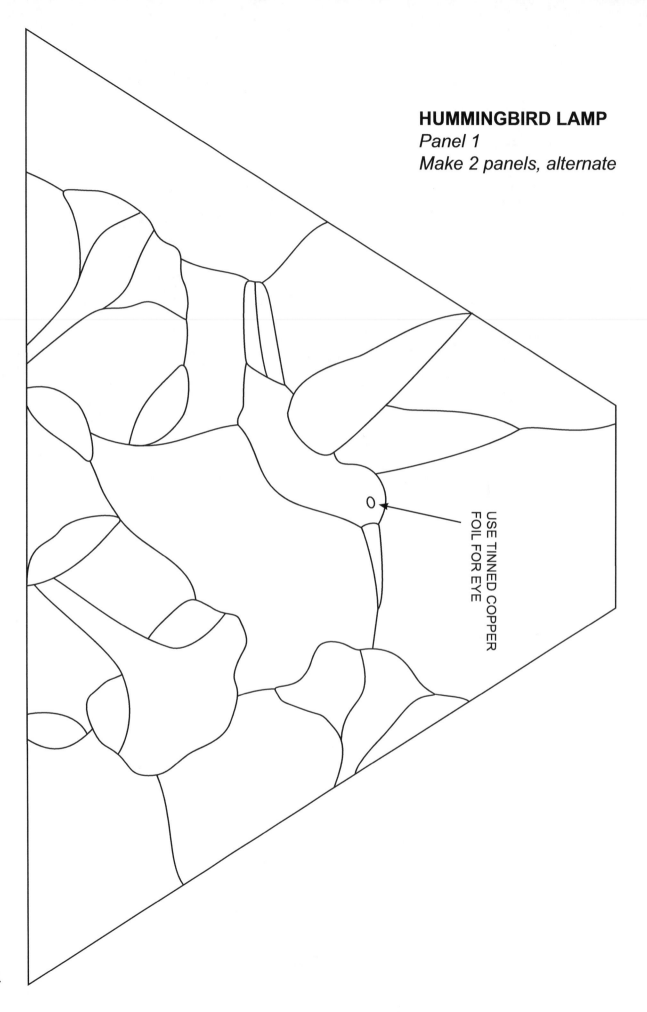

HUMMINGBIRD LAMP
Panel 1
Make 2 panels, alternate

USE TINNED COPPER
FOIL FOR EYE

4

HUMMINGBIRD LAMP
Panel 2
Make 2 panels, alternate

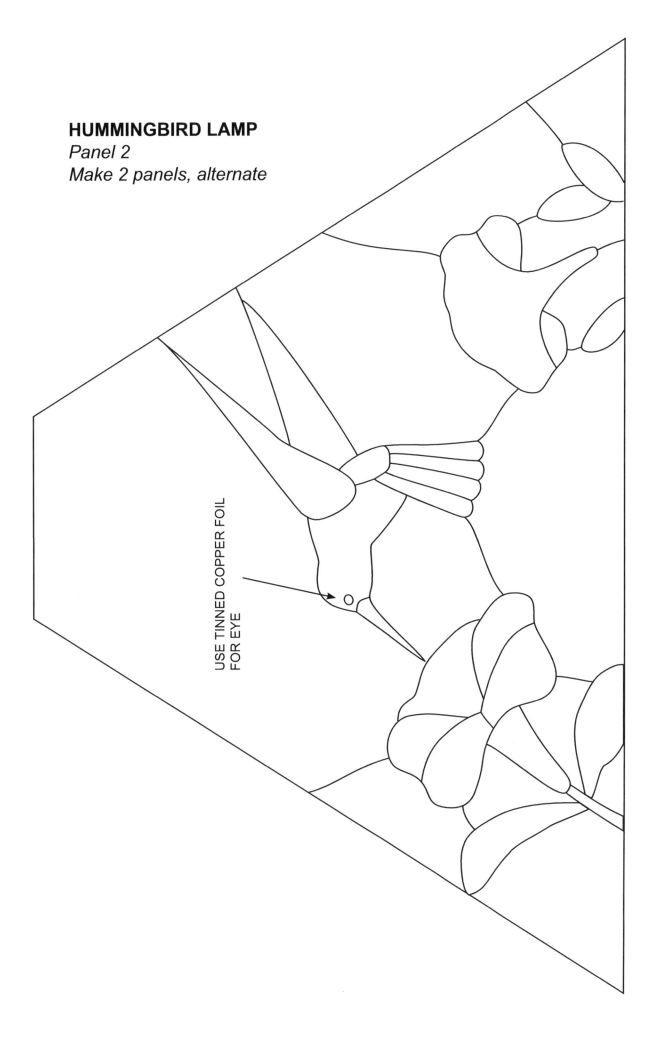

USE TINNED COPPER FOIL FOR EYE

5

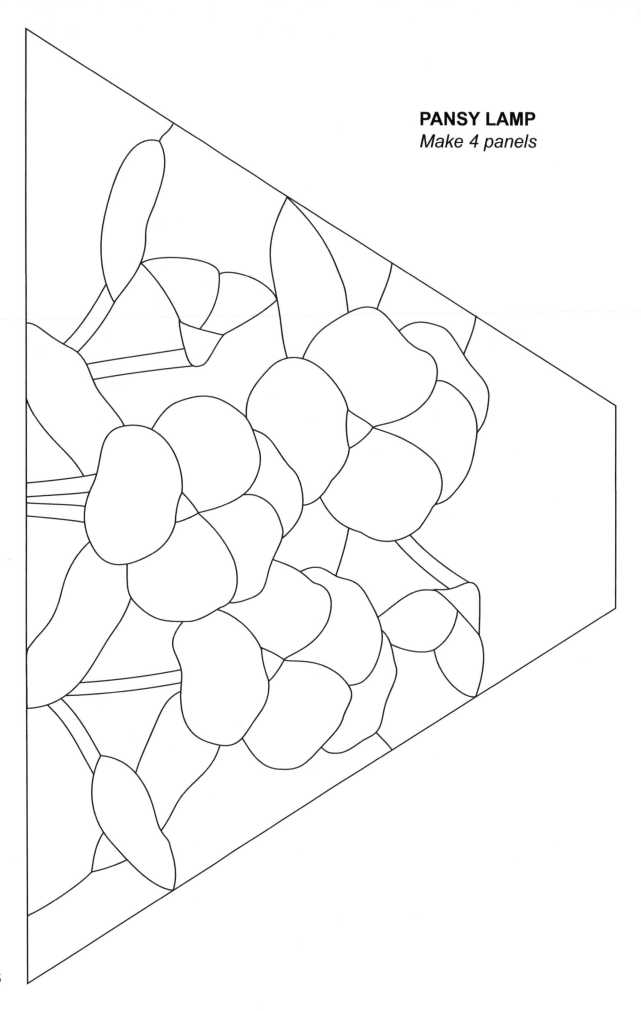

PANSY LAMP
Make 4 panels

6

IRIS LAMP
Make 4 panels

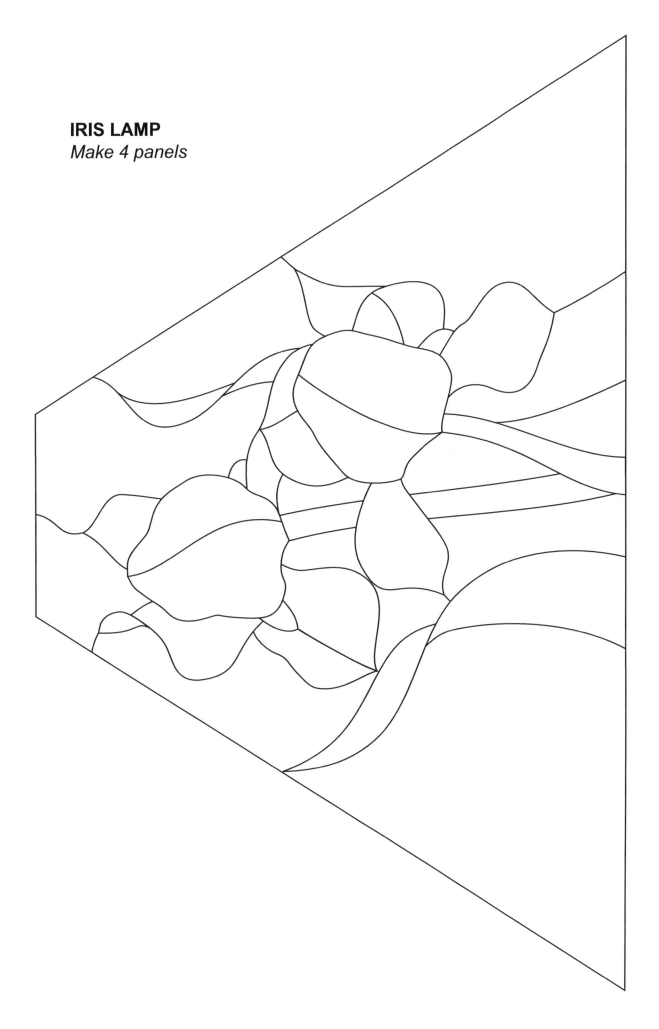

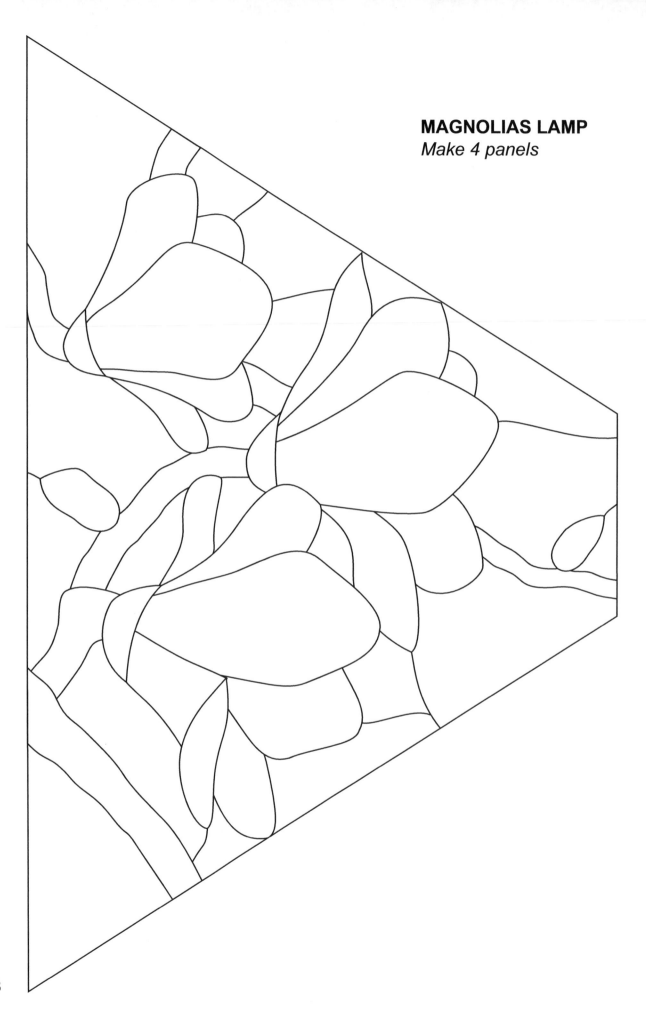

MAGNOLIAS LAMP
Make 4 panels

8

WATER LILY LAMP
Make 4 panels

9

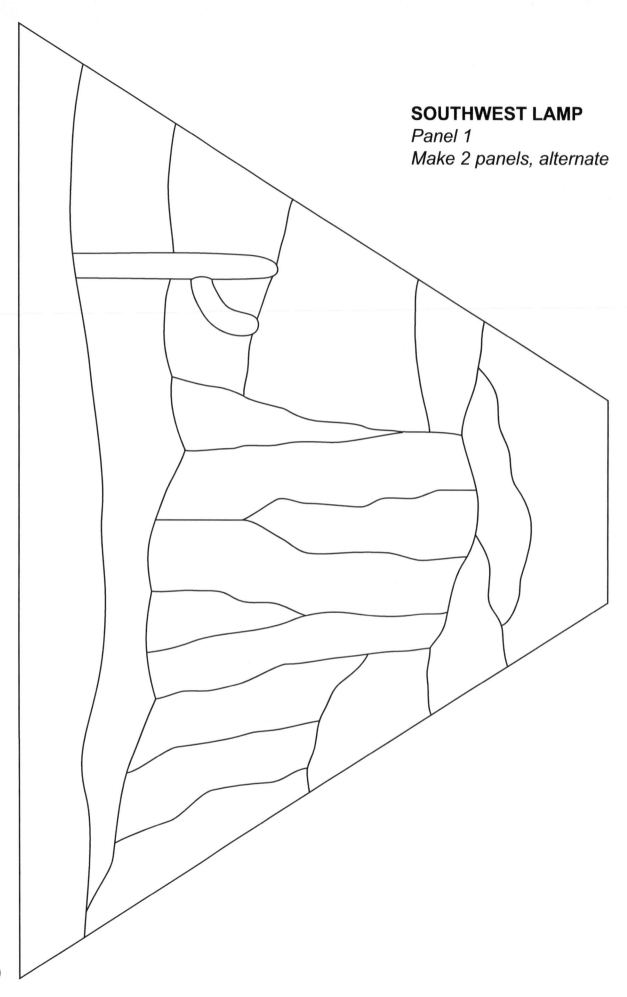

SOUTHWEST LAMP
Panel 1
Make 2 panels, alternate

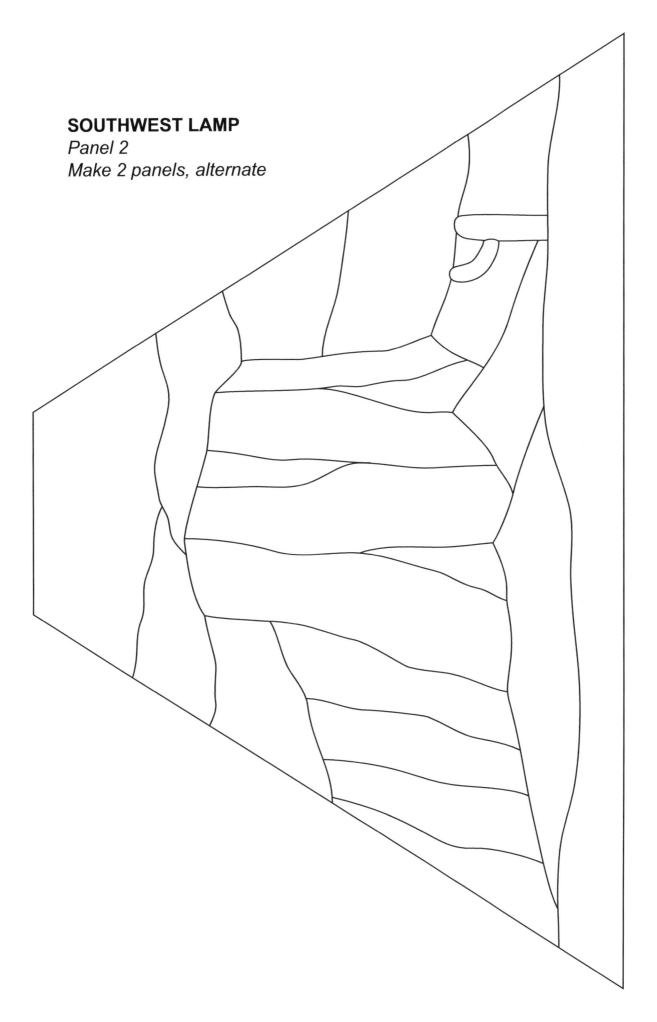

SOUTHWEST LAMP
Panel 2
Make 2 panels, alternate

11

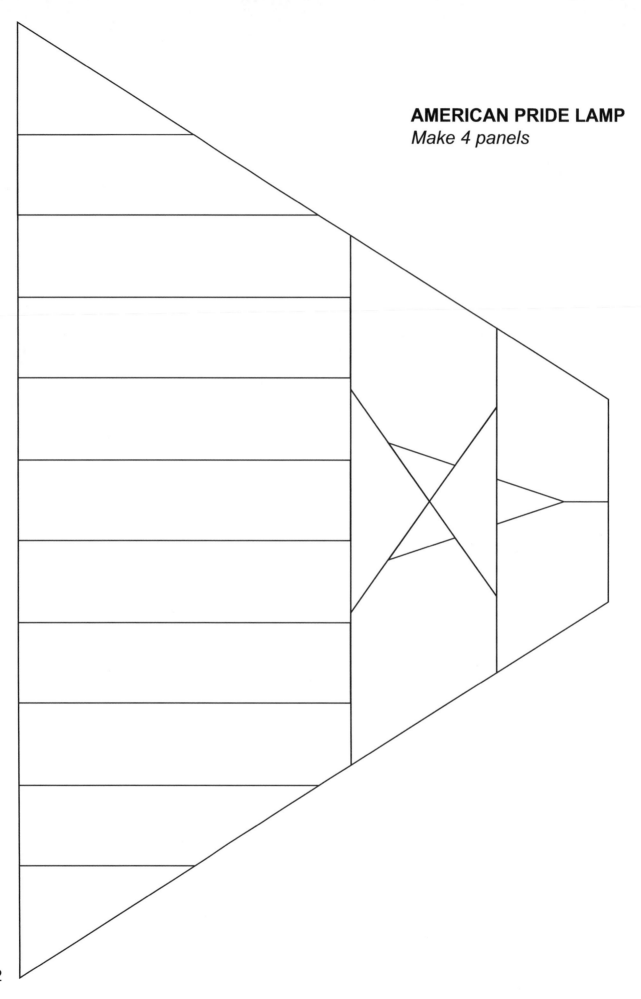

AMERICAN PRIDE LAMP
Make 4 panels

12

DAYLILIES LAMP
Make 4 panels

WIRE STEMS

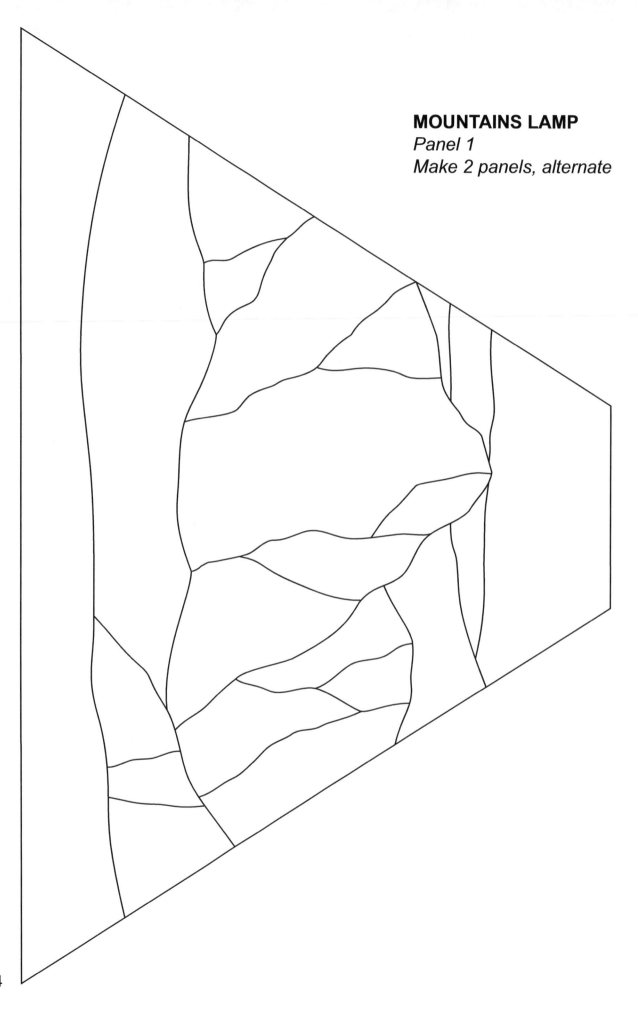

MOUNTAINS LAMP
Panel 1
Make 2 panels, alternate

14

MOUNTAINS LAMP
Panel 2
Make 2 panels, alternate

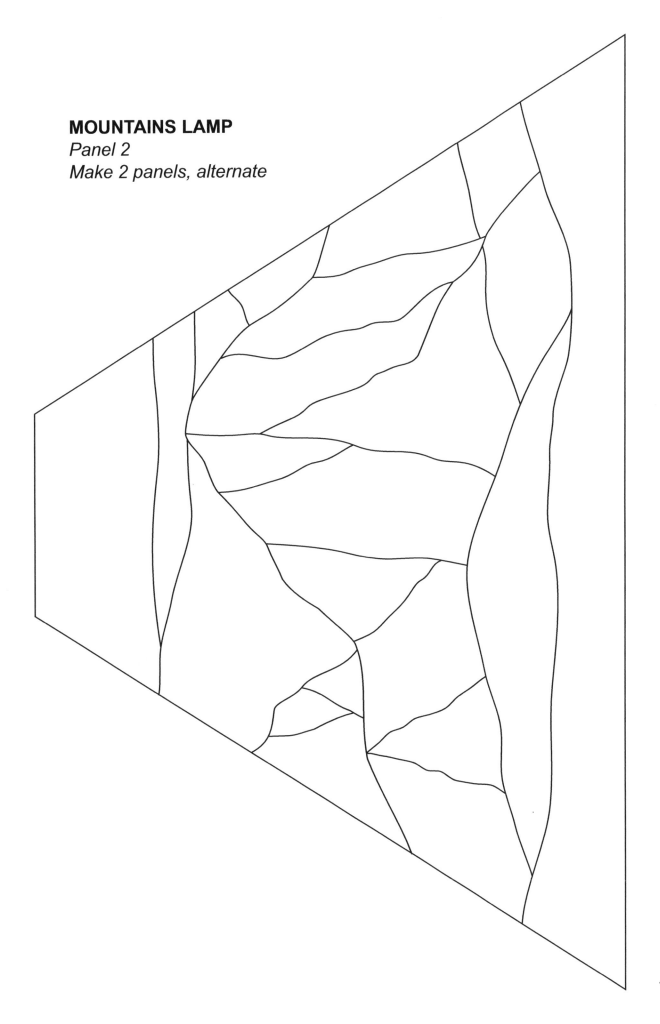

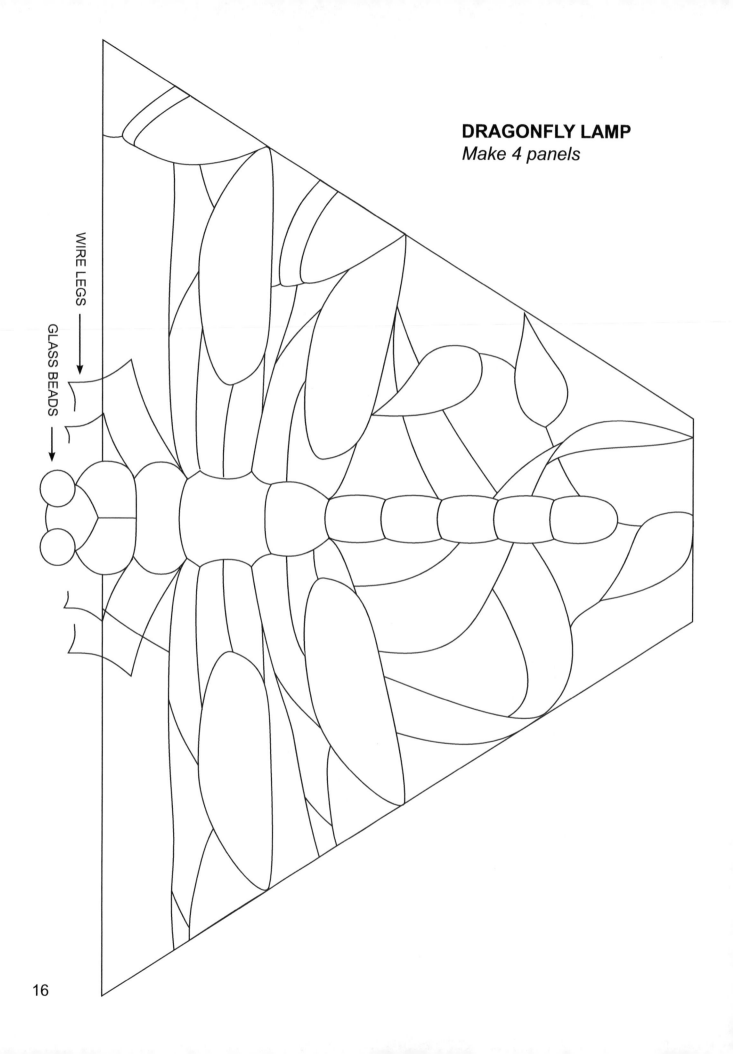

DRAGONFLY LAMP
Make 4 panels

WIRE LEGS →

GLASS BEADS →

16

POINSETTIAS LAMP
Make 4 panels

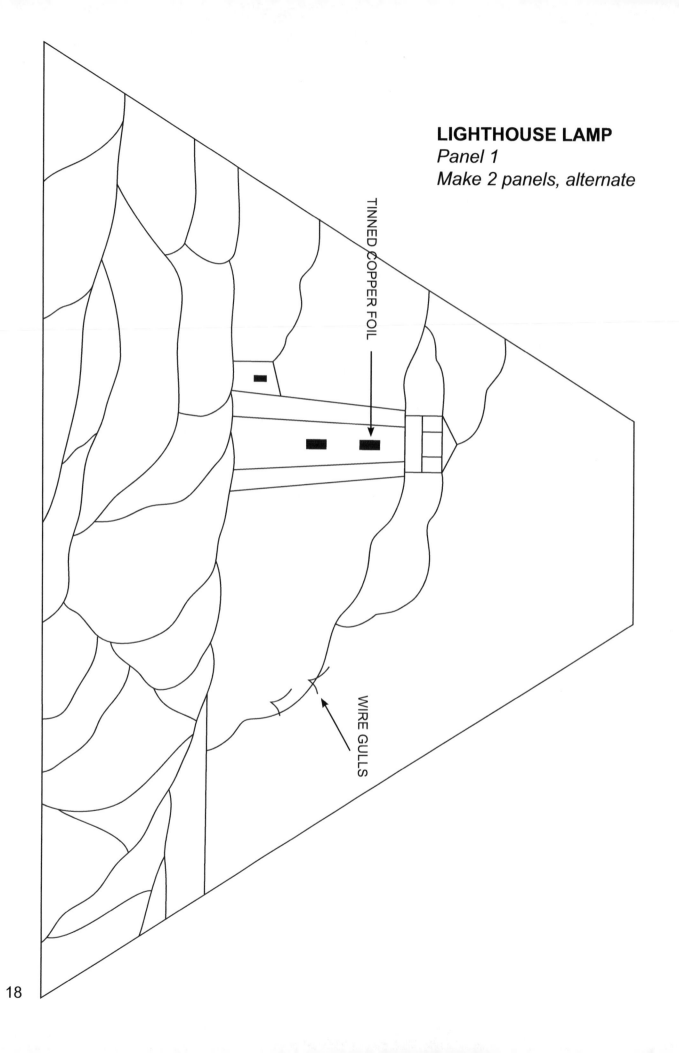

LIGHTHOUSE LAMP
Panel 1
Make 2 panels, alternate

TINNED COPPER FOIL

WIRE GULLS

18

LIGHTHOUSE LAMP
Panel 2
Make 2 panels, alternate

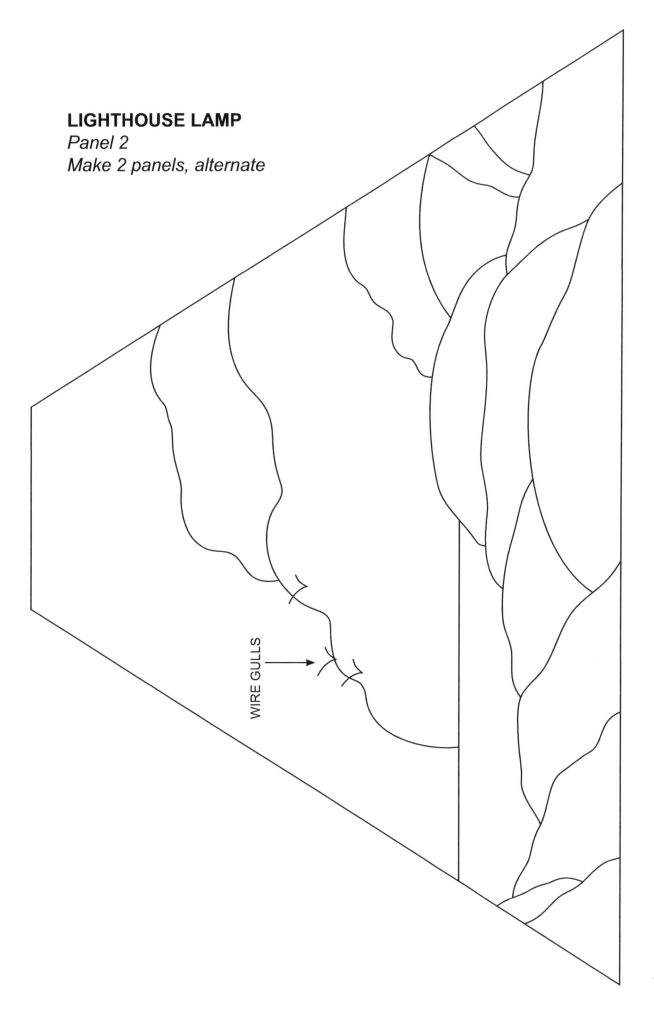

WIRE GULLS

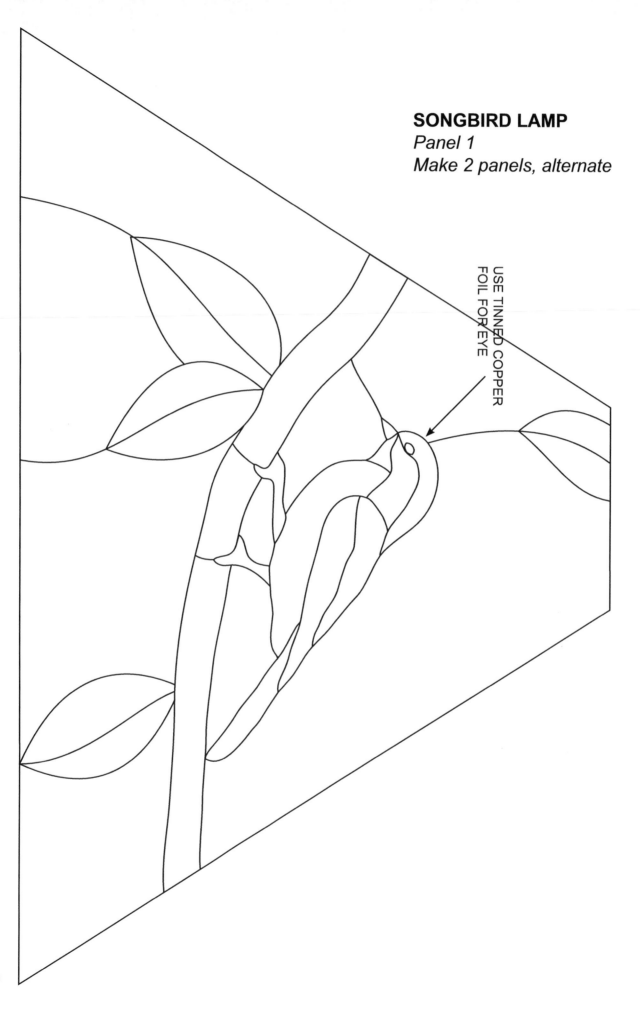

SONGBIRD LAMP
Panel 1
Make 2 panels, alternate

USE TINNED COPPER FOIL FOR EYE

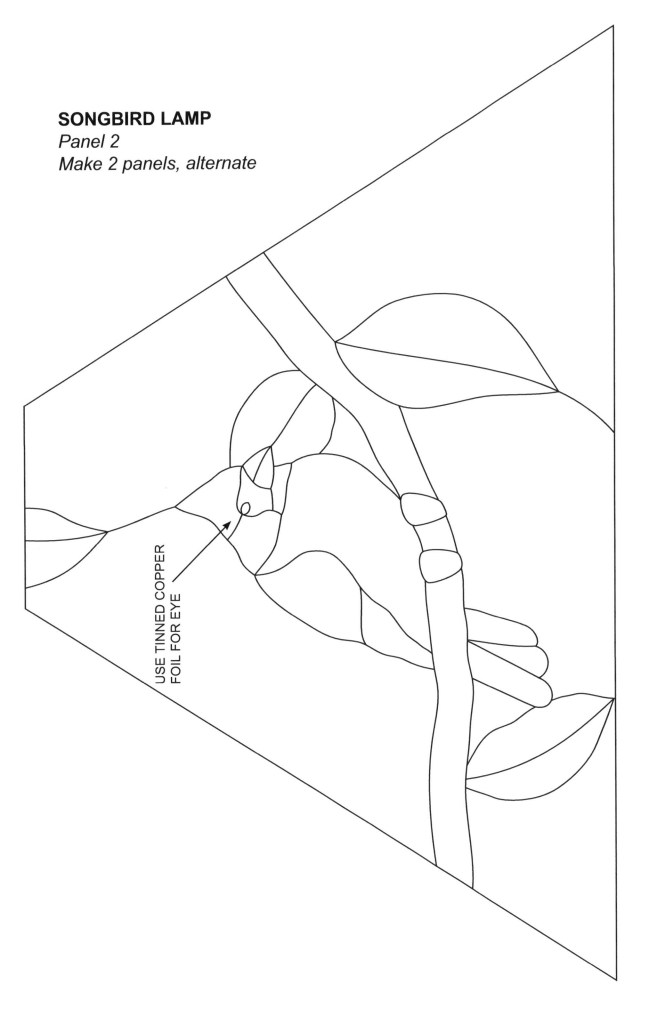

SONGBIRD LAMP
Panel 2
Make 2 panels, alternate

USE TINNED COPPER
FOIL FOR EYE

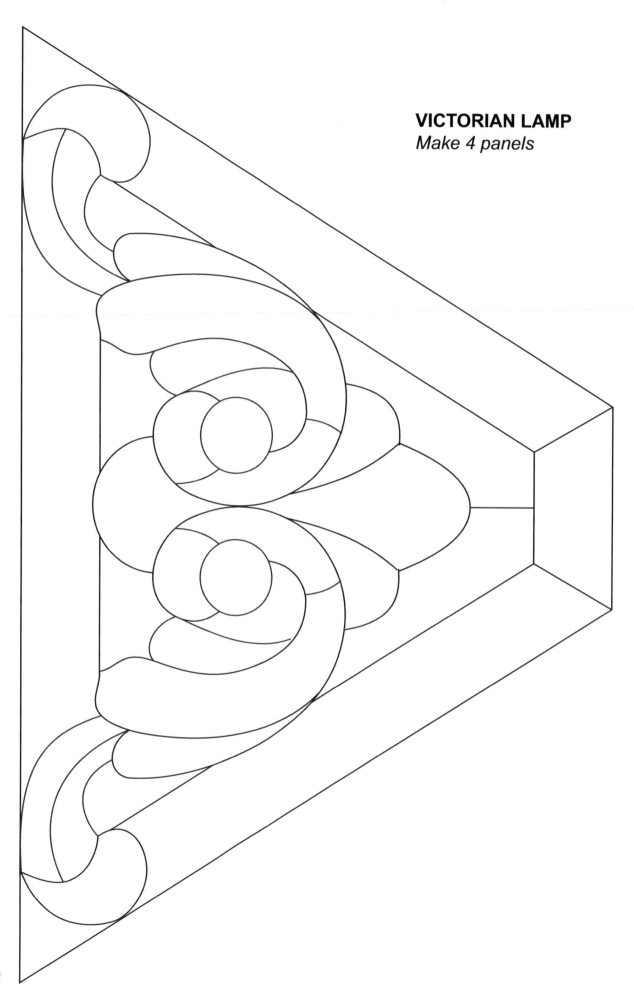

VICTORIAN LAMP
Make 4 panels

22

ART NOUVEAU LAMP
Make 4 panels

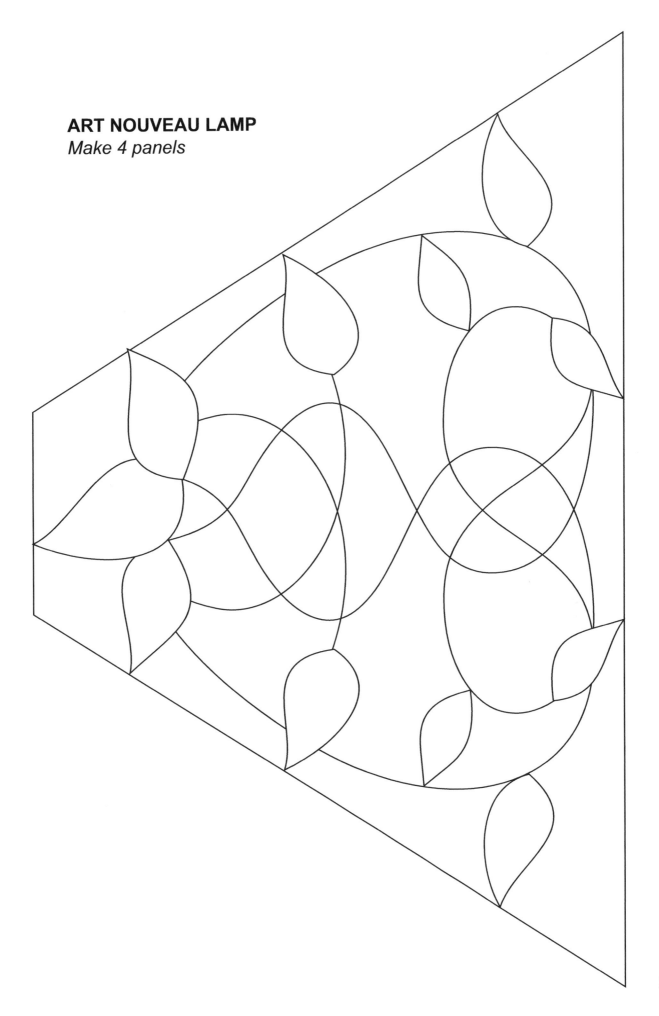

BOOKS AND OTHER PRODUCTS AVAILABLE
FROM CLIFFSIDE STUDIO

Visit our website at www.cliffsidestudio.com
Also available at Amazon.com

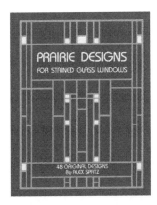

Prairie Designs for Stained Glass Windows

10th Anniversary Edition with 8 new designs for a total of 56 original Prairie window designs in a variety of sizes and shapes.

Prairie Designs II

The sequel to "Prairie Designs for Stained Glass Windows" features 48 new Prairie window designs in a variety of sizes and shapes.

Prairie Lamps

18 full size patterns for 12" square Prairie lampshades. Designs match certain windows in "Prairie Designs" book. Instructions included for enlarging designs to 14" and 16" lampshades.

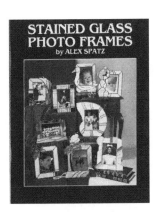

Stained Glass Photo Frames

20 full-size assorted patterns for 4" x 6" and 5" x 7" photo frames.

Photo Frame Lights

Over 30 designs of this unique hinged photo frame. One side of the frame holds a photo and the other side is a design panel with a night light.

Also available from Cliffside Studio

- **Patterns**
- **Vase Caps**
- **Lamp bases**

PRODUCTS AVAILABLE FROM CLIFFSIDE STUDIO
Visit our website at www.cliffsidestudio.com

Made in the USA
San Bernardino, CA
03 July 2016